DATE DUE			

WHY TURTLES HAVE SHELLS

ISBN 0-89868-525-7–Library Bound
ISBN 0-89868-526-5–Soft Bound
ISBN 0-89868-527-3-Trade

A PREDICTABLE WORD BOOK

WHY TURTLES HAVE SHELLS

Story by Janie Spaht Gill, Ph.D.
Illustrations by Bob Reese

 ARO PUBLISHING

A turtle had no shell in
the days of long ago,

and so he had no warm dry
home like turtles as we know.

His name was Timothy Turtle and he took a walk one day,

to see if he could find a place warm and dry to stay.

5

He came upon a bear cave. He
thought, "that cave will surely do."

So he asked the warm, dry bear,
"may I live with you?"

"My home is big," said the bear, "for a turtle a cave won't do.

You need to find a smaller home that's exactly right for you."

He came upon a bird nest.
He thought, "that nest will surely do."

So he asked the warm, dry bird, "may I live with you?"

"My nest is high." said the bird,
"for a turtle a nest won't do.

You need to find a home on the
ground that's exactly right for you."

He came upon an ant pile. He
thought, "that pile will surely do."

14

And so he asked the little ant,
"may I live with you?"

"My hole is tiny." said the ant,
"for a turtle a pile won't do."

"You need to find a larger home that's exactly right for you."

Walking along the shore,
Timothy saw an empty shell.

He thought, "that shell could keep me
warm and dry. I think it would work well.

That shell is not too big, nor too
small, that shell is not too high.

20

I think that it would work just fine.
I'll put it on and try."

Timothy found that turtle shell
did keep him warm, and dry.

Now all the turtles wear a shell,
and that's the reason why.